Beyond Grief
to acceptance and peace
2nd Edition

SIMPLE, PRACTICAL THINGS YOU CAN DO
TO HELP YOURSELF AND YOUR FAMILY
THROUGH THE GRIEVING PROCESS

By AMELIA E. POHL
with
consulting psychologist
BARBARA J. SIMMONDS, Ph.d.

EAGLE PUBLISHING COMPANY OF BOCA

Copyright © 2000, 2001 by AMELIA E. POHL
Third Printing 2002
All rights reserved.

No part of this book may be reproduced or transmitted for any purpose, in any form and by any means, graphic, electronic or mechanical, including photocopying, recording, or by any information storage or retrieval system, without permission in writing from AMELIA E. POHL.

EAGLE PUBLISHING COMPANY OF BOCA
4199 N. Dixie Highway, #2
Boca Raton, FL 33431

Printed in the United States of America

ISBN 1-892407-47-7 SECOND EDITION
Library of Congress Catalog Card Number: 2001091065

The purpose of this book is to provide the reader with an informative overview of the subject. This book is sold with the understanding that neither the publisher nor the authors are engaging in, nor rendering medical, psychiatric, accounting, legal or any other professional service. If you need medical, psychiatric, accounting, legal, or other expert advice, then you should seek the services of a duly licensed professional.

WEB SITES: Web sites appear throughout the book. These Web sites are offered for the convenience of the reader only. Publication of these Web site addresses is not an endorsement by the authors, editors or publishers of this book.

This book is intended for use by the consumer for his or her own benefit. If you use this book to counsel someone about the law, accounting, psychology, psychiatry or medicine, then that may be considered an unauthorized and illegal practice.

The Consulting Psychologist

BARBARA J. SIMMONDS, Ph.D., a noted psychologist, has collaborated with the author on those sections of this book dealing with the grieving process. Dr. Simmonds has been practicing in the field of Health/Rehabilitation Psychology and Gerontology for the past 10 years.

Her experiences in the field led her as a natural outcome to develop expertise also in Grief Counseling, since so many losses accrue to individuals in a health care setting.

In addition to her work in hospitals, nursing centers and private practice, Dr. Simmonds has served as Adjunct Faculty at Nova Southeastern University, teaching courses in Aging, Stress Management and Grief Counseling.

Dr. Simmonds holds a Master's Degree in Gerontology and a Ph.D. in Clinical Psychology from Nova Southeastern University. She was the Director of Psychological Services at Villa Maria Nursing and Rehabilitation Center for eight years and now continues her relationship with the institution on a consultation basis. She continues with her private practice in North Miami, Florida.

About the Author

Before becoming an attorney in 1985, AMELIA E. POHL taught mathematics on both the high school and college level. During her tenure as Associate Professor of Mathematics at Prince George's Community College in Maryland, she wrote several books including Principals of Counting, Probability: A Set Theory Approach, Common Stock Sense.

During her practice of law Mrs. Pohl observed that many people want to reduce the high cost of legal fees by performing or assisting with their own legal transactions. She found that, with a bit of guidance, people are able to perform many legal transactions for themselves. Attorney Pohl is utilizing her background as teacher, author and attorney to provide that "bit of guidance" to the general public in the form of self-help books that she has written.

Her latest project is a series of books that explain the legal and practical things a person needs to do when someone dies and how to set up your own Estate so that property is passed quickly and at little cost.

Because the laws of each state govern what needs to be done to settle an Estate, the book is state specific, meaning that the author is writing a different book for each state. Each book in the series is co-authored by an attorney from that state. In the event the reader has a specific question, he can be referred to that attorney. The name of the series is *Guiding Those Left Behind*.

Books in the series are now available for the following states:

ALABAMA		ARIZONA
CALIFORNIA		FLORIDA
GEORGIA	ILLINOIS	INDIANA
MARYLAND		MASSACHUSETTS
MICHIGAN		MINNESOTA
MISSISSIPPI		MISSOURI
NEW JERSEY		NEW YORK
NORTH CAROLINA		OHIO
PENNSYLVANIA		SOUTH CAROLINA
TENNESSEE		TEXAS
VIRGINIA	WASHINGTON	WISCONSIN

The rest of the series is scheduled to be printed in 2003.

Beyond Grief
to acceptance and peace

contents

chapter		page
1	Grief Before Death	*11*
2	The Grieving Process	*21*
3	Helping a Child Through the Loss	*33*
4	The Adult Orphan	*51*
5	Strategies to Cope with the Loss	*55*
6	The Problem Death	*67*

You need to experience the pain and walk through it, rather than to avoid it.

You need to go down the path of grief to get beyond it.

Hopefully, this book will make your walk a little easier.

Grief Before Death 1

Approximately ten percent of deaths occur suddenly because of accident, suicide, foul play or undetected illness. For the rest, dying is a slow, gradual process taking several months, and in many cases years. It is the reverse of being born. A birth begins with the gleam in the eye of the parent. From there the embryo grows in strength and development until that painful progression through the birth canal culminating with the child's first breath of fresh air.

Death is that process in reverse. Instead of gradual growth there is gradual decline with the loss of vision, hearing and mobility as the body ages. Systems begin to shut down. As the nervous system shuts down, moving is restricted. Walking becomes difficult. As the digestive system shuts down the person becomes unable to eat. Finally the respiratory and circulatory systems quit. The heart stops beating, breathing ceases and the spirit departs, to return to a gleam in the eye of his maker.

People think that the grieving process does not begin until that moment of death, but in many cases the grieving process begins when one day we acknowledge to ourselves that the one we love is old, and will probably not be with us much longer. Maybe that is why so many of us dislike old age. Not only do we grieve the loss of those we love, but also of ourselves. To look in the mirror and see an old person before you is to know that you have started that gradual decline.

Not everyone chooses to acknowledge the decline, either in themselves or others. Why be sad now and later? May as well wait until there is something to worry about. And besides with all of these medical advances, who knows how long anyone will live? This cheerful optimist begins the grieving process only when their loved one is actually dead, and buried. It may take that long for the fact of death to sink in.

Most others begin the grieving process when a loved one comes down with a life-threatening disease such as terminal cancer, end stage Alzheimer's disease, or a progressive disease of any of the major organs (heart, liver, kidneys, etc.). Grieving prior to the death differs from the grieving process that occurs once a person dies in that the person is often unaware that they are grieving. It is only after the death that they may look back and recognize that they experienced grief before the death.

Many go through grieving stages similar to those experienced by people once the person actually dies, namely:

- ➢ shock, disbelief
- ➢ sadness, depression
- ➢ loneliness
- ➢ anger, guilt
- ➢ acceptance

That is what Paul experienced when he learned that his mother had been diagnosed with Alzheimer's disease. There was initial disbelief "This can't be right. We've never had this problem in our family. Let's get a second opinion."

When the diagnosis was confirmed, Paul was sad to the point of depression. Sad for his mother, sad for himself. Concerned that he may have inherited a tendency for the disease. He did not mind declining physically – but mentally, that was something else. What a terrible way to go.

As the disease progressed, his mother withdrew into herself. Finally, Paul was no longer able to communicate with his mother. He missed being able to pick up the phone and talk to her. He missed the holiday gatherings and her good home cooking. He missed having a mother. He never remembered having any heart to heart talks with her. Still he knew she was always there for him; and now that relationship was over.

13

As the years passed, Paul visited his mother less and less. His sister thought Paul didn't care for his mother as much as she did. But the truth was that Paul was distancing himself from his mother because it was too painful to watch her in the end stages of the disease. Each visit would leave Paul upset and depressed.

Yet staying away didn't seem to help either. Paul felt that he was abandoning his mother. He felt guilty about leaving the job of caretaking to his sister.

When his mother finally died, Paul did not grieve. He had already been through the grieving process and had long since accepted the fact of his mother's death.

Paul was lucky to go through the grieving process only once. Sometimes a person grieves before the death and then all over again after the death.

That was the case with Debbie. She described her marriage to Jerry as a 50-50 relationship. Half the time she loved him and half the time she wished she never met him.

They had been married for over thirty years. Maybe that was the problem. They knew each other so well that each was master at pulling the other's strings. And yet somehow they stayed together. In the beginning it was "for the sake of the children." Later it was because they had been together so long that neither knew how they would function as a single person. Besides there were no serious problems. No infidelity. No spousal abuse. No drug addiction (except for Jerry's smoking). The problem wasn't that the marriage was bad, the problem was that it wasn't all that good.

When Jerry came down with lung cancer, Debbie had trouble accepting the diagnosis. Sure she had always been on his case about smoking. She often lectured "How can you, a man with a college education, be so stupid as to smoke when you know how bad it is for you?" Yet when the doctor told them that he had a "spot" on his lung, she wouldn't believe it was cancer until she saw the biopsy report and had to accept the diagnosis.

The doctor was encouraging. He said it was in the early stages. He outlined a program of chemotherapy and radiation. What he did not say was how much of a drain the treatment would be on both of them. At first Debbie was solicitous. Hovering over Jerry. Seeing to his every comfort. But as the months passed she grew irritable.

Although the initial treatment was successful, within the year the cancer returned. The doctors treated the cancer more aggressively than before but Jerry only got worse. He became too weak to work. He was around the house all day long, and the couple soon got on each others nerves. Jerry was always complaining about something or another. But mostly it was the illness. He felt sick and he was having a hard time dealing with it.

Debbie didn't feel well herself. She felt a tightness in her chest. Every little noise bothered her. Sometimes she felt breathless and would often sigh. But mostly she felt exhausted. She went for a general checkup, but the doctor found nothing physically wrong. He suggested that the stress of caring for her husband was causing her to feel irritable and depressed. He recommended she speak with a psychiatrist.

She came away from her visit to the doctor angry. How could he suggest that she had mental problems? Her problem was Jerry!

But in fact, she was angry at herself. She should have left him when he was healthy. He was hard enough to live with under the best of conditions. Now she was finding her 50-50 marriage was more 60-40. But how could she leave him now that he was so sick? She felt trapped, helpless.

The house began to look like a nursing home with Debbie the full time nurse. Helping Jerry from the wheelchair to the bed; feeding him pills every day; arranging oxygen apparatus. She hated every minute. Her only consolation was "It can't last much longer." But the months passed and Debbie became increasingly angry, depressed and filled with guilt at not being more compassionate with her dying husband.

Even Jerry's physician could see that Debbie was about at her breaking point. He said "There isn't much more that I or you can do for Jerry. All we can do is see that he is free of pain and in a peaceful and comfortable environment. I doubt whether he has more than a few days to live. I think we should move him to Hospice. That will make things easier on both of you."

"I can't afford expensive nursing care."

"No, Medicare pays for Hospice care."

Debbie was hesitant "I don't know how Jerry is going to handle the move. Isn't that the same as telling him he is going to die?"

17

The doctor reassured her "I think Jerry already knows that he is dying. If he hasn't come to terms with that fact, then Hospice can help. And they can help you as well. You call your local Hospice and they will explain their program to you. If you are hooked up to the Internet then you can get information by using your search engine and typing in the word "HOSPICE."

The doctor encouraged Debbie to talk it over with her husband. "If Jerry wants to stay home, then we can arrange to have the Hospice people visit you here at home."

Debbie was surprised when Jerry said he thought it was a good idea to go into the Hospice facility "This is too much on you. We'll both be more comfortable there."

Debbie dreaded the trip to Hospice. She did not know what to expect, but it was a place for dying, so it had to be dreary. What a surprise when she entered the facility. She must be in the wrong place. It looked like a country club. Everyone seemed cheerful and pleasant. Didn't they know people were dying here?

Jerry's room was also cheerful and bright, with a large window that looked out over a wooded area. The first thing the Hospice workers did was to see to it that Jerry was comfortable and in no pain. The Hospice counselor came each day. She explained that dying is both a physical and spiritual process. A gradual letting go of the body and a detachment from worldly things.

She helped Jerry and Debbie to understand that even though they both knew on an intellectual level that Jerry was dying, neither had been able to accept the fact of his death.

The Hospice counselor helped them work through some of their problems and encouraged them to acknowledge their fears and concerns. For the first time Debbie was able to admit that a large part of her anger was directed at Jerry just because she was angry that he was dying and going to leave her. She was concerned about how she would manage once she was all alone. She said she was worried about her future.

19

Jerry made her laugh when he said "Your future? What about my future? I'm the one who's dying here. How do I know what's coming? I'm not so sure that there is an afterlife. And if there is a hereafter. How do I know where I am headed?"

Finally Jerry and Debbie were able to say good-bye. One of the last things Jerry said to Debbie before he died was "You haven't been the best wife and I haven't been the best husband. But you are my wife and I am your husband and there always has been love between us."

It would be nice to end this story saying that Debbie did all of her grieving before the death and was able to be at peace once Jerry died, but that isn't what happened.

She continued to grieve for months thereafter. She had much regret. The guidance offered by the Hospice counselor had helped them so much. It made Debbie sad to think how much happier they might have been had they both worked to improve their marriage.

When Jerry died she grieved the loss of what she had. More than that, she grieved the loss of the marriage that she didn't have.

The Grieving Process 2

The funeral is over.

Everyone went home.

You experienced and got past the initial grief.

All the affairs of the decedent have been settled.

But is the grieving over? Do you have closure? To use a tired expression, have you been able to "get on with your life" or do you find that you are still grieving?

And how about the children?
How are they taking the loss?

The death process is not over until the family finds peace and acceptance of the loss.

Psychologists have observed that it is common for a person to go through a series of stages as part of the grieving process. There is the initial shock of the death and often disbelief and denial:
"He can't be dead. I just spoke to him today!"

It is common for a mourner to be angry — angry at the decedent for dying — angry at a family member for something he should or shouldn't have done — just plain angry.

Sometimes an ill person is aware of his impending death and becomes angry, as if mourning his own death. Relations with the family may become strained under the stress of the illness. If there was an argument with the decedent, the bereaved may be left with an unresolved conflict and feelings of guilt.

Mourners often experience guilt. Many have an uneasy feeling that the death was somehow their fault. Some regret not having spent more time with the decedent. Others feel guilty because they weren't present when the decedent died.

There is grieving even when death is long expected and even welcomed. This was the case with a wife who nursed her husband at home for nine long years. Her husband suffered from debilitating strokes, a chronic heart condition, and finally failing kidneys. She often said "Some things are worse than death."

When he died she was shocked. He had been so close to death so many times. Each time he pulled through. She couldn't believe he died. And that wasn't the only surprise. She was surprised at the depth of her emotions. She thought she would be relieved. She didn't think she would experience such intense grief.

If she thought about it she would have realized that grieving is not intellectual. It is emotional. She knew in her head that his death was best for both of them, yet there was this empty space in her heart. It took her a long time to get through the grieving process.

THE STAGES OF GRIEVING

Although professionals in the fields of psychiatry and psychology have observed that guilt and anger are stages of grieving, there is no agreement about the number or composition of the stages of grieving. This is not surprising. The ways people react to death are as diverse as there are people. Some people seem not to grieve at all. Whether such people experience any stage of the grieving process may not be known even to the person himself.

And there is diversity in grieving even in the same person. Each circumstance of death in one's life is different from another, so a person will grieve differently when different people in their life die. But for purposes of this discussion, we note that many people who lose someone they love report experiencing the following emotions and in the following sequence:

- ➤ initial shock, disbelief, alarm
- ➤ numbness, anger, guilt
- ➤ an intense longing for the deceased
- ➤ sadness, depression, loneliness
- ➤ recovery, acceptance of the loss, peace

With the exception of the intense longing, these are much the same emotions as people experience who have gone through the grieving process prior to the death.

COPING WITH THE LOSS

How the general population deals with the death of a loved one was investigated in 1995 by the AMERICAN ASSOCIATION OF RETIRED PERSONS ("AARP"). AARP asked National Communications Research to conduct a telephone survey of over 5,000 people aged 40 or older. Approximately one third of the respondents reported that they had experienced the loss of a close friend or family member within the past year. Those reporting a loss were asked to describe specific coping activities that they had engaged in since the death of their loved one.

    67% reported talking with friends and family
    16% read an article or book about how to cope with death
    9% received help with legal or practical arrangements
    5% attended a grief support group

When asked what strategies they found to be most helpful in coping with their loss:
    28% said talking with a friend or family member was most helpful
    24% said their religion was most helpful
    10% said knowing it was for the best
    6% said memories of the deceased
    4% reported staying busy as the best strategy.

It is interesting to note that 67% of the people turned to their family and friends yet only 28% reported this as being most helpful to them.

Many times friends and family members want to help but they are at a loss as to what to say or do. The next section discusses different techniques that can be used to help with the grieving process.

Family and friends want to help the person who is grieving, but sometimes they don't know how to do it. They may feel just as helpless in dealing with the loss as does the bereaved — not knowing what to say to console those grieving.

There are no magic words, but saying you are sorry for the loss is appropriate and generally well received. Avoid platitudes such as: "It was fate." "It was God's will." "It was for the best." Especially avoid telling the bereaved that you know how he/she feels. People who suffer a great loss do not believe that anyone can understand how they feel; and they are probably correct. It is better to tell the bereaved what you are feeling:
  "I was shocked when I heard of the death."
  "I am so sad for you."
  "I am going to really miss him."
Knowing that you share the feeling of loss is comforting to someone who is grieving.

The wake or funeral is not the time to express curiosity about how property is to be distributed. Statements such as "I gave that imported glass vase to your mother; and I was wondering whether she remembered to tell you to give it to me" are at best tacky, if not downright insensitive.

Listening is more important than talking to the bereaved. They may need to explore the circumstances of the death — how the person died; where and when he died, etc. They may need to express what they are feeling, whether it be grief or anger. Try not to change the subject just because you are uncomfortable with the topic or with the expression of emotion.

If the bereaved wishes to reminisce about the decedent, then join in the conversation. Talk about the decedent's good qualities and the enjoyable times that you shared together.

If during the funeral period, you want to do something such as prepare food or send flowers, then consider asking the bereaved for permission to do so. The family may prefer donations to a favorite charity in place of flowers. The family may have already made dinner plans for the guests.

Do not make general offers of assistance.
 "Let me know if you need anything" is not likely to get a response even if the bereaved does need help with something. A better, more sincere, approach is a specific offer, such as, "If you need transportation, I can drive you to the cemetery."

Your assistance during the post-funeral period is more important than during the funeral period. During the funeral the bereaved is usually surrounded by family and friends and has more than ample assistance.

Any offer to help at that time may not even register because the bereaved may be numb with grief and unable to comprehend what is going on around them. In many cases they are unable to even recall who was present at the funeral, nonetheless who offered to assist them.

Once the funeral is over and everyone has gone home, that is the time to offer support. The bereaved needs to go through a transition period and must learn to live without the presence of their loved one. In general, the more dependent the bereaved was on the decedent, the more difficult the transition. In such case, you can be most helpful if you are able to offer assistance with those tasks of daily living that the bereaved is not accustomed to performing.

For example, if the decedent was the sole driver in the family, then you might help the bereaved to learn to drive or at least help find public transportation. If the decedent handled all of the family finances, you might assist the bereaved in bill paying and balancing a checkbook. If math is not your forte, help to find a bookkeeper who can assist for a reasonable fee.

But, the best thing that family and friends can do for the bereaved, is just to be there for them. As shown by the AARP survey, the specific coping activity used by the majority of the bereaved was to talk to a friend or relative. A telephone call, or a card, on a special anniversary or on a holiday will be appreciated. You can help most with a call or a visit. It is just that simple.

Also be patient with the bereaved. There is no set time to get through the grieving process. It may take considerable time for the mourner to be able to find some quality of life. But if several months have passed and you are concerned that the bereaved is still not functioning well, you might consider suggesting that the bereaved seek assistance. Try not to be judgmental when making the suggestion. Don't say
"You're not helping yourself get through this,"
but rather,
"I can see that you are still having a hard time getting through this difficult period. Have you considered seeing _____?"

Suggest whatever is appropriate to the mourner. For example, if the mourner is a religious person, then suggest a visit with his/her religious leader. If the mourner is a social person, then suggest a support group. If the bereaved is severely depressed, then a visit to a doctor or psychiatrist may be the best recommendation.

Do not expect your recommendation to be well received. The mourner may become angry or annoyed that you even made the suggestion. It may be difficult for the mourner to accept the fact that he/she needs assistance. Some people, mostly men, think it an admission of weakness to agree that they need help. They believe they should be able to "tough it out."

Some mourners may have increased their consumption of alcohol or turned to drugs in an attempt to deal with the pain that they are experiencing. If they accept your suggestion, they may need to deal with a growing addiction, in addition to the problem of overcoming the grief, and they may not be willing to do that.

Elderly people might think there is a stigma associated with any kind of counseling. They may insist "There's nothing wrong with me" fearing that you think they are unbalanced or somehow mentally defective.

Some people, especially the overachiever type, refuse to seek counseling because they perceive asking for help to be a sign of failure — an admission that they failed to work out the problem themselves. It's as if they failed "Grieving 101."

But those most resistant to a suggestion of a need for counseling are mourners who use denial as a defense mechanism. They may brush off the suggestion with "No. I'm alright" or "I'm doing a lot better" even as tears well up in their eyes.

If they deny that they are having trouble getting past the grief, then they do not need to deal with the problem. If they deny that they have a problem, then they don't have the problem; and that solves that!

In such cases, the timeworn adage, "You can lead a horse to water, but you can't make him drink," applies. The mourner needs to take the first step himself. You cannot take it for him. All you can do is assure the mourner (and yourself) that you have confidence that he/she can, and will, work this through.

Helping A Child Through The Loss 3

The first thing parents observe about their second child is how very different that child is from their first child. Parents quickly learn that each of their children is an individual, with his/her own separate response to any given situation. It is important to keep this fact in mind when trying to assist a child through the loss of a close family member or friend. Because each child is different, there is no single proper way to assist a child through a period of mourning. You can help the child most if you consider the child's background as it relates to the loss:

What is the child's relationship to the decedent?

What were the circumstances of the death?

Was it expected or was it sudden or tragic?

What is the emotional age of the child?
That age may differ significantly from his/her chronological age.

For example, consider the family of Harold and Elaine, parents of three children. Emily, the eldest child, was one of those "born old" children, wise beyond her years, sensitive and shy. Her brother John, two years her junior was the direct opposite — boisterous, immature, constantly in motion. Peter came along five years later. He was the baby of the family, a cherub, always smiling, indulged by parents and siblings.

When their paternal grandfather died, Emily was 10, John, 8 and Peter, 3. Their parents expected the death because "Gramps" had been suffering from cancer for a long time. No mention was made to the children of the serious nature of the illness, so Emily was surprised to learn of the death. She shed no tears but retreated to her room and soon became occupied with a computer game.

John and his father cried together when they were told that Gramps had died. Gramps was both kind and generous with a great sense of humor. Best of all he was never critical of John's rambunctious behavior. It seemed to John and his Dad that they lost the best friend they ever had.

Peter did not understand what was going on; but he reacted empathetically, patting John on the shoulder, and saying "Don't cry Johnny."

When it came time to go to the funeral Emily refused to go. Johnny got angry with Emily for something or another and pushed her down. She was not hurt, but she cried loudly and carried on. Peter started whining. The whole day was hard on their parents.

The next few months were equally difficult. John woke up with nightmares. Emily was sullen and withdrawn. No one mentioned the death except Peter who was full of questions:
"Where's Gramps?"
"Was he in that box?"
"Where did they put the box?"
"Why was everyone crying?"

Harold and Elaine were having their own problems dealing with the loss and they had no patience with the children. The family eventually got back to normal, but it might have been easier on all of them had the parents prepared the children for the dying process.

PREPARING FOR THE EVENT

Most deaths are expected. The majority of people who die are ill for several months before their death. Children are not always aware of a family member's mortal illness so it comes as a shock to them when it happens. It might have been easier on Emily and John if their parents said something like:

Gramps is old and very ill. It happens that all living things, plants, animals and people, eventually die. No one knows for sure when someone will die, but it may be that because he is so old and so very sick that Gramps may die sometime within the year.

If either child wanted to pursue the subject, then that could lead to a discussion of the funeral process:

When someone dies in our family, all of our friends and family gather together to talk about how much we loved the person and how much we will miss having that person with us. Later we go to the gravesite where we say prayers and our last good-byes.

It is important for parents to explain the children's role in this process, but like most couples, Harold and Elaine never thought about, much less discussed, their children's participation in the funeral and burial service. Had her parents told Emily what to expect and what was expected of her, she might not have objected to attending the funeral.

Before discussing the matter with the child, it is important that a husband and wife explore their own views on their children's participation in a funeral and burial. They may find that they have differing views on the following issues:

What factors should determine whether a child attends the wake and/or funeral:
⇨ custom or convenience?
⇨ the age and emotional maturity of that child?
⇨ the relationship of the child to the decedent?

Should the child be allowed to decide whether he/she wishes to attend the wake and/or funeral?

Should a child be allowed (or encouraged) to touch or kiss the corpse?

Should children participate in grave site ceremonies?

Should a child be encouraged or required to visit the grave site at a later date?

37

There are no right or wrong answers for any of these questions. Each family has its own set of customs and values and the answers to these questions need to conform to those customs and values. What is important is that the couple agree about what they expect of their children and then impart that expectation to their children.

The "imparting" is the difficult part. No one likes to talk about death. Parents have been told that they need to discuss sex with their children. They have been told that they need to discuss drugs with their children. These are important, life threatening, issues but it is entirely possible that a child will grow to be an adult without ever having someone close to them die. So why bring up the subject?

The reason to discuss the matter is the same reason to discuss sex with your children. The sex they see on television or hear about from their friends is a reflection of societal values but perhaps not your family values. You discuss sex to impart your family values and expectations to your children. If you wish to express to your children your views on the dying process, and your belief about an afterlife, then it is appropriate to discuss these matters when you believe the child is sufficiently mature and ready for the discussion.

Maybe the best time to discuss death with the child is when someone close to them is quite aged or seriously ill. If they heard that some family member is dying, they may have concerns or questions that you can answer. Most children fear the unknown and death is an unknown to them.

Of course, children are aware of the fact of death almost as soon as they can speak. It is all around them. Animated characters "die" as part of a computer game. Children's cartoon movies and television shows contain death and dying scenes. A child may have a pet that dies. Children hear about people dying almost nightly on the news.

Although children are familiar with the concept of death, they do not know how they or their family will react to the death of a loved one. If the topic is discussed prior to an impending death, the child may find it comforting to know what to expect, what behavior is expected of them, and what choices they may have regarding their attendance at a wake or funeral.

AFTER THE FUNERAL

Once the funeral is over, you need to deal with your own loss. That may be a difficult process for you so you may not even notice that your child is also grieving. This was the case with Harold and Elaine. They were not aware that Emily was having a difficult time with the loss — after all she didn't even cry when she heard of the death. Had they thought about it, they may have realized that Emily was retreating into herself. Her continued sullen attitude should have signaled that she was having difficulty coming to terms with the loss.

Had her parents encouraged Emily to talk about the problem, they would have learned that she was ambivalent about her relationship with her grandfather. She loved him, but she felt that he favored her brothers. Gramps always played "boy" games of catch and touch football. He never took the time to get to know Emily and she resented that. Now that he was gone, there would be no opportunity for her to have a meaningful relationship with her grandfather.

People are helped most by talking with a friend or relative about their loss. The same applies to children. Emily could have profited had she been able to explore her feelings with either of her parents. Her parents might also have profited because they may have developed a closer relationship with Emily and established a pattern of open communication.

As it was, Emily never did resolve the problem. Her parents suffered her sullenness without ever a clue as to what Emily was all about. Unfortunately, this lack of communication continued as Emily grew older and ever more a closed book.

John fared better. Harold recognized that John's nightmares were related to the loss. Harold made an effort to spend more time with the boy and not to be so critical when John acted up.

As for Peter, his parents tried to answer his questions as best as they were able. Elaine had the uneasy feeling that she was not answering them "the right way." She thought she made a mistake by saying that "Gramps is now at rest" because Peter asked if Gramps was sleeping. She thought that she might have caused Peter to confuse death and sleep.

41

If Elaine investigated she could have found any number of excellent publications dealing with the subject. Many funeral homes provide families with complimentary pamphlets on how to answer children's questions about death. The local library and bookstore have any number of excellent publications designed to answer questions raised by small children.

Most religious organizations offer printed material for young people that explain death from the organization's perspective. For religious families, this is a good opportunity for the family to discuss their religious beliefs as they relate to the loss of a loved one.

Today's child is computer literate. A child may, on his own, decide to seek an E-mail buddy to work through a problem the child may be having with the death. Parents need to supervise such communication because the child may be especially vulnerable at this point in his/her life.

Many Web sites offer publications relating to the issues of death and dying. You can use your favorite search engine to locate such sites. See the next page for Web sites that offer information and counseling services for children who have suffered a loss.

INTERNET RESOURCES

GRIEFNET   http://www.griefnet.org
Griefnet is a Web site that offers E-mail support groups. **KIDSAID** is a companion site to GriefNet offering peer support groups for children who are dealing with a loss.

❦❦❦❦❦❦❦❦❦❦❦❦❦❦❦❦❦❦❦❦❦

New England Center   http://www.neclt.org
for Loss & Transition
New England Center for Loss & Transition is a non-profit organization. Its companion site **THE COVE**, is a support program for grieving children and their families.

❦❦❦❦❦❦❦❦❦❦❦❦❦❦❦❦❦❦❦❦❦

RAINBOWS   http://www.rainbows.org
RAINBOWS is a not-for-profit international organization offering training for those who wish to establish a peer support group. Their companion site **PRISM** is a support group for single parents and stepparents.

❦❦❦❦❦❦❦❦❦❦❦❦❦❦❦❦❦❦❦❦❦

HOSPICE NET   http://www.hospicenet.org
HOSPICE NET is a comprehensive Web site that offers information about hospice services, caregivers, patients and counseling for children who have experienced a loss.

THE TROUBLED CHILD

Most deaths are from natural causes. The death is expected and not all that difficult for the family to finally accept. The *problem death* is one that is tragic, unexpected, and/or a death that cuts short a life. More and more school officials are recognizing that the loss of a member of the school community deeply affects the student population. Many schools have adopted a policy of having school psychologists counsel the students as soon as the death occurs. They do not wait until a school child shows signs of being disturbed by the event.

It would be well for parents to adopt the same policy. Specifically, if your family suffers a problem death, consider seeking the services of a professional who is experienced in grief counseling just as soon after the death as is practicable. The next day is none too soon.

A case in point was that of a 14 year old girl who lived with her grandmother, a jovial, robust woman whose main pleasures in life were eating and telling funny stories. One morning when they were having their usual breakfast of fried eggs, sausage and buttered toast, the grandmother complained about her doctor and how the doctor was on her case about losing weight and lowering her cholesterol. She no sooner finished the sentence when she suffered a heart attack. She died within minutes.

That was a problem death. The death was both unexpected because the grandmother looked quite healthy. It was tragic because it occurred in the presence of the granddaughter.

No one knew how deeply this affected the girl until a few months had passed. The girl was losing quite a bit of weight. When questioned, she said that it was over-eating that caused her grandmother's death and she wanted to be sure that she ate a healthy diet with absolutely no fat. Concerned family members explained that losing too much weight was just as bad as being overweight. The girl agreed with them, but she continued to lose weight.

When family members realized the severity of the problem they took her to a doctor, who in turn referred them to a psychiatrist. The diagnosis was anorexia, triggered by the loss of the only person in the child's life that she felt close to.

Unfortunately, no amount of therapy, antidepressant, or medical intervention helped.

The girl died a year later.

A death does not always need to be a problem death to cause a problem for a child. If a child has unresolved issues with the decedent, then that child may need professional assistance in coping with the loss. Children do not manifest grief or depression in the same way as adults, so look for changes that are atypical of the child and that do not resolve themselves within a reasonable time after the death.

Consider consulting with a child psychologist if your child exhibits unusual or antisocial behavior:
- eating too much or too little
- destructive or aggressive behavior
- sleeping too much or too little
- misbehaving at school
- a sudden change in school performance

The red flag, signaling an immediate need for counseling, is a child who talks or writes about committing suicide. It is important to act quickly to show the child that you understand that he/she is having a rough time and that you and the doctor are going to assist the child with the problem.

There are any number of resources in the community to assist the child, from school counselors to religious organizations. For those who cannot afford private care, counties offer low-cost services on an ability to pay basis. Some religious organizations offer counseling services to their members, as well as to the general public, on a sliding scale basis.

Before seeking counseling services, it is important to schedule a physical checkup for the child. There is a chance that the problem is physiological. Some illnesses cause behavioral changes; for example, food allergies can cause aggressive behavior. Hearing or visual deficiencies can cause a child to withdraw into himself. Even infections can cause behavioral disturbances. Perhaps the child is on drugs and an examination should pick that up. All these things need to be ruled out prior to counseling.

If your child has been treated by the physician over the years, the doctor may know the child well enough to be able to offer some insight into the problem. If the checkup does not reveal a physical problem, the physician may be able to suggest the right type of treatment, i.e., psychologist or psychiatrist, and perhaps give you a referral.

CHOOSING THE RIGHT COUNSELOR

There was a film called GOOD WILL HUNTING in which a brilliant, but troubled, teenager was required, by court order, to attend counseling. The funniest part of the film was the manner in which the boy went through counselors. He deliberately alienated (and was alienated) by many doctors until he met the right one for him. Similarly, if your child needs counseling you might need to interview several counselors before you find someone with whom your child can work; someone who speaks on his/her level — someone the child can trust.

The issue of trust may create a dilemma for the parent. The child is the counselor's patient. The counselor cannot betray the child's trust by revealing what was said during treatment, yet parents need to know whether the treatment is helping the child. The counselor can, and should, disclose to the parent the diagnosis, prognosis and type of proposed treatment. The parents need to employ someone they trust to pursue the course of treatment that they determine is best for their child.

In seeking a counselor, personal references are the best avenue, although it may be difficult to find a friend or relation who has had his/her child successfully treated for a similar problem. With or without references, you need to investigate the counselor's background. What is his/her training? What percentage of the practice is devoted to children in this age group? Is the counselor experienced in working with children who are having difficulty coping with the loss of a loved one?

Interview more than one counselor before making your choice. If the child is sufficiently mature and able to cooperate in choosing the right counselor, then that is an important step forward. If not, you may need to be assertive and go with the counselor whom you trust and are most comfortable. If it turns out that there is no improvement within a few months, then you need to find another counselor. As with the student in GOOD WILL HUNTING, it may take several tries before you come upon someone who can help your child.

The Adult Orphan 4

The baby boomers are a unique group in many ways. What other group has transition periods marked by headlines? "Baby Boomers Turn 50" is the latest newsworthy event. The "Adult Orphan" is a condition unique to that age group. Most Boomers have had their parents with them for half a century. Their parents have survived longer than any other generation in recorded history. But now the Boomers' parents are in their 80s and 90s and Boomers will need to learn to live without them.

For some this is no big deal. For others it is overwhelming. That was the case with two sisters. Opposites from birth. Patti was an independent spirit. Rebellious, strong-willed, she left her hometown to go to college and never looked back. She didn't even resemble her sister Maria. Maria was short, dark-haired, with a bit of a weight problem. Patti looked like an aging flower child with long, straight hair. You'd hardly pick them out as sisters, except for their resemblance to their parents. Patti had her Dad's angular features (especially his sharp nose) and Maria, her mother's soft round features.

51

Maria lived within 10 miles of her parents all her life. It was a great shock when her Dad died suddenly of a heart attack. But her mother was there to comfort her and offer her words of encouragement, even though her Mom was struggling with the loss herself. That was Mom's way. Always putting the needs of her children before her own.

Patti was the strong one at Dad's funeral. Making the funeral arrangements. Greeting family members. Helping Mom to settle Dad's estate. She seemed to know exactly what needed to be done and how to do it.

Maria seemed as dependent as Patti was independent. Maybe it was Maria's personality. Maybe she was raised that way. Maybe her parents needed Maria to need them as much as Maria needed to lean on them.
"Co-dependent" taunted Patti.

How Maria hated that phrase!

Maria never thought of herself as being dependent. She married and raised two children of her own. Over the last few years she took care of her mother as her mother's health failed. Maria's whole day revolved around her mother; making sure she was fed and comfortable.

Maria did not know how she would fill her days now that her role of caretaker was over. But the emotional loss was the hardest part. Her mother had been her closest confident, her best friend.

Maria held up better at her mother's funeral than she had expected. It was Patti who seemed to fall apart. When Maria thought about it, she understood. Her parents gave Patti unconditional love. Patti found that nowhere else. All other relationships in her life were flawed. Her two marriages ended in divorce and that bothered Patti greatly. Bad enough to make a mistake once. How could she have been so stupid as to pick two losers? Yet her parents neither condemned nor lectured. They were there for Patti emotionally and financially. They were her safety net. Now they were both gone.

At the funeral Maria looked over at her sister. Patti seemed lost, like a motherless child, an orphan. Patti would need to grow old without the support of her parents.

Now she would need to grow up.

Strategies to Cope With The Loss 5

Once a person accepts the fact that their loved one is dead, they are past the initial phase of the grief process. Most people do very well and are able to go through the remaining stages with no overt effort on their part. Others suffer profoundly and need to find ways to get through the grieving process. If you have recently experienced a loss and are having difficulty coping with the loss then consider your own personality type and explore those strategies that might help you through.

Do you enjoy socializing with people or do you prefer solitary activities?

Are you a "do-it-yourself" type of person or do you feel more at ease with someone leading you through the process?

STRATEGIES FOR THE PRIVATE PERSON

If you find socializing to be difficult, then consider non-social activities such as reading a self help book. There are many excellent publications that explore the grieving process and how to adjust to the loss.

MEDITATION
Praying or quiet meditation may offer you consolation. This may be a good time to explore different kinds of meditative techniques. You can find books on meditative techniques such as Zen or visualization in the Philosophy section of the library or bookstore. You can find books and videos on Yoga in the exercise section.

GET A COMPUTER BUDDY
If you are computer literate, you can participate in an Internet support group. An anonymous chat room may be just the thing to help you express the loneliness and sadness you are experiencing.

You can locate E-mail support groups for people who are dealing with all types of grief issues by using your favorite seach engine. You can find such groups by searching topics such as:
    GRIEF   MOURNING   DEATH   DYING

THINK NEW THOUGHTS

Private people tend to be "thinkers." Grieving is an emotion accompanied by sad thoughts. Replacing the sad thoughts with other thoughts can ease you through the grieving process. It's much like distracting a fussy child. The way a mother turns tears to smiles is to distract the child with "Oh, look. Teddy bear needs some tickling!" Your mother is not here to distract you. But now that you are an adult and you have the maturity and skills to distract yourself.

To think new thoughts you need to be spontaneous. Instead of doing the same old thing everyday, think of something to do that is different. It could be something as simple as going out for breakfast instead of fixing the same bowl of cereal and starting the morning with the same heavy heart.

Expectations also lead to sadness. You might expect family members to behave in a certain way. Maybe you expect someone to call or visit you more often. And of course they don't, so you become hurt, angry, sad. By giving up expectations over which you have no control, you can avoid setting yourself up for sad thoughts. And whenever possible try not to dwell on small things that annoy or frustrate you. Such emotions often lead to sadness. Try to think of the bigger picture. Whenever possible, replace negative thoughts with "This is not important. It just doesn't matter."

STRATEGIES FOR SOCIAL PERSON

If you are a social person, then consider using those types of activities that involve a social setting, such as joining a bridge, bowling or golfing group. If your grief is too deep to concentrate on recreational activities, consider joining a support group. The power of the support group is companionship. They offer the one thing you may need most at this time — just someone to listen.

If you belong to an organized religion or a civic organization, find out whether they have a support group for people who are going through a grieving process. If your organization does not have a support group, then consider starting one yourself. It can be as simple as putting a notice in a weekly bulletin that you are holding a meeting for anyone who lost a loved one within the past year. You can hold the meeting as part of a picnic or barbecue with everyone bringing a dish for others to share. Just getting together and sharing experiences may help you and others in your organization as well.

If you do not belong to an organization, then look in the newspaper for notices of meetings of local support groups or consider joining one of the many national support groups. Web sites for some well established national groups appear on the next two pages.

PARENTS WITHOUT PARTNERS, INC.
1650 South Dixie Highway, Suite 510
Boca Raton, FL 33432   (561) 391-8833

PARENTS WITHOUT PARTNERS is a national non-profit organization for single parents. They offer group discussions and single parent activities such as picnics and hikes. Their national headquarters is in Florida. They can direct you to the chapter nearest you.

PARENTS WITHOUT PARTNERS WEB SITE
http://parentswithoutpartners.org
E-mail: pwp@jti.net

LOSS OF A PET

Those who suffer the loss of a pet may experience a sense of loss similar to the loss of a close family member. Often they hesitate to turn to friends or family members (especially those who never owned a pet) believing they just wouldn't understand.

Some local Humane Societies provide a pet loss counseling service. Some veterinarian medical schools have volunteer counseling services. There is a list of pet grief counseling services on the Internet:

http://www.superdog.com/

59

AMERICAN ASSOCIATION OF RETIRED PERSONS

AARP GRIEF AND LOSS PROGRAM
WIDOWED PERSONS SERVICE   (800) 424-3410
601 E Street NW
Washington, DC 20049

AARP has support groups for widowed persons throughout the United States. They also have support groups for adults who have suffered the loss of a family member such as a parent or sibling. You can call the above number and they will let you know if there is a support group in your area.

AARP WEB SITE
http:// www.aarp.org/griefprograms
E-mail: griefandloss@ aarp.org

THE PHYSICAL ASPECTS OF GRIEF

Accompanying the emotional stages of grief, are physical symptoms that mourners commonly experience:
- tightness in chest, shoulders or throat
- over sensitivity to noise
- breathlessness, causing the person to sigh
- dry mouth
- muscular weakness
- loss of energy, fatigue

These symptoms may be experienced even with people who are going through the grieving process in anticipation of the death. Such was the case in the example given on page 16. Very often doctors will attribute the symptoms to the stress of caring for a loved one who is seriously ill. But in many cases, it is just part of the grieving process.

It is just as important to deal with the physical aspects of grieving as it is with the emotional. People who suffer extreme grief tend to become extreme in everyday activities. They may forget to eat. Some find themselves eating all day. Some develop sleep disturbances and go without sleep for long periods of time while others suffer the opposite extreme of wanting to sleep all day.

If you find that your grief is affecting your physical well being, then it is important to make a conscious effort to care for yourself:

✭ EAT A BALANCED NUTRITIONAL DIET

Contrary to popular taste, sugar, salt, fat and chocolate do not constitute the four basic food groups. And contrary to current food faddism, no one diet fits all. The ability to digest certain foods varies from person to person and we all have ethnic preferences. You need to learn what balance of fats, protein (meat, fish, legumes) and carbohydrates (fruit, vegetables, grains) you require to maintain your optimum weight and state of well being; and then make an effort to keep that balance in your daily diet.

✭ GET SUFFICIENT REST

There is much variation in the amount of sleep required from person to person. You know how much sleep you normally require. Try to maintain your usual, pre-loss, sleep pattern. If you are finding difficulty sleeping at night, resist the urge to sleep during the day. It is easy to reverse your days and nights. Awake all night, dozing all day, will only make you feel as if you are walking around in a fog.

✯ EXERCISE EACH DAY

Exercise can be as simple as taking a brisk 20 minute walk, however the more sustained and energetic, the greater the benefit. If you are having trouble sleeping at night, try exercising during the late afternoon and eating your main meal at lunch rather than late at night.

Eating right, getting sufficient sleep, exercising — most people have heard these recommendations from so many sources (doctors, psychologists, writers for health magazines, etc.) that they seem to have become a cliche. But the reason that so many professionals make these suggestions is simply that they work. Doing all these things will make you feel significantly better.

And this may be the time for a complete physical checkup. Grieving is hard on the body. The cause of your physical discomfort may not be emotional. It could be that there is a medical problem that needs attending.

ADJUSTING TO A NEW LIFE STYLE

If you lost a member of your immediate family, then in addition to going through the stages of the grieving process, you need to go through a transition period in which you learn how to live without the decedent. The child must learn to live without the guidance of a parent. Parents may need to put their parenting behind them. The spouse must learn to live without a partner, and as a single person.

In addition to learning to live with the loss, the bereaved may need to establish a new identity. Such was the case with Claire. She and Fred were married 44 years when he died after a lengthy battle with cancer. At first Claire didn't think she could live without him. She had been a wife for so long. She had trouble thinking of herself as a single person — nonetheless being one.

Claire had difficulty accepting the fact that Fred was dead, even though she expected he would die for months before he did. She would see Fred in her dreams. Sometimes she thought she saw him sitting in his favorite chair. When Fred appeared to Claire, he looked the same as when they were first married. Sometimes she thought he was speaking to her.

What was most comforting to Claire was that Fred was smiling at her. She was relieved to know that Fred was no longer in pain and was at peace. The smile on his face was a relief to her because she feared he might be angry with her for the many times he would call out her name and she would become annoyed with him. She felt guilty that she did not have more patience as a caregiver.

Claire found herself talking to Fred especially during those times that she was undecided as to what to do. As time progressed, she began to incorporate her husband's beliefs into her own so that instead of asking herself "What should I do?" it became "This is what Fred would have done."

Eventually Claire found that she was able to function on her own. She began to re-engage with the world. She found new interests to pleasantly occupy her time. She learned how to live as a single person. She is now more self sufficient than at any other time in her life. She laments that Fred no longer visits her.

She still misses him.

Claire was able to get beyond the grief. She did it on her own, though she will tell you that she did it with Fred's help.

Claire's case is not unusual. As verified by the AARP survey, most people adjust to the loss on their own, requiring only an assist from family and friends, but there is a percentage of the grieving population who require assistance and need to seek professional grief counseling.

For those experiencing psychological problems prior to the death, the event of the death may be the precipitating factor to mental illness requiring treatment. Similarly, if a person had a drinking problem or a drug addiction before the death, the event of the death may exacerbate the addiction.

Some deaths are so violent or tragic, that even the sturdiest may be unable to resume their life without professional assistance. In the next section, we discuss ways of coping with the problem death.

The Problem Death 6

We defined the problem death as one that is unexpected, tragic or a death that cuts short a life. Such a death is an immediate problem in terms of the funeral, burial and estate settlement, but the most difficult problem is getting through the mourning period.

The death of a child is always a problem death. Even if the child is an adult, the parent experiences extreme grief. No one expects to outlive his or her child. In these days of a lengthening life cycle, more and more parents may come to experience such a loss. The loss may come at a time when the parent is frail or in poor health, making it all the more difficult to deal with the loss.

The only thing harder than losing an adult child is losing a young child. Nothing compares to the intensity of grief experienced by a parent when a little one dies. Some parents believe they are losing their mind. Many feel that their lives can never have meaning again. They suffer guilt and recrimination "Maybe I could have prevented it." There is even guilt for returning to ordinary living. If the parents find themselves smiling, laughing or making love they think, "How can we be doing this? How can we ever be normal again?"

The family who experiences a tragic or violent death should consider seeking professional grief counseling as soon as practicable after the death. The grief counseling can be in the format of a self-help group. Participants profit from talking and sharing with others who understand what they are experiencing.

There are many specialized self-help groups that provide literature and peer support for families who experience a problem death.

FOR PARENTS OF MURDERED CHILDREN

THE NATIONAL ORGANIZATION OF
PARENTS **O**F **M**URDERED **C**HILDREN, INC.
National Chapter
100 East Eighth Street, B-41
Cincinnati, OH   45202   (888) 818-POMC

POMC has support groups and contact people in each of the fifty states. You can contact the National Chapter for the group nearest you.

　　　　　　　http://www.pomc.com
　　　　　　　E-mail   natlpomc@aol.com

Beyond Grief to Acceptance and Peace

FOR PRENATAL OR NEONATAL DEATHS

M.E.N.D. **M**ommies **E**nduring **N**eonatal **D**eath
P.O. Box 1007   (888) 695-MEND
Coppell, TX   75019

MEND provides monthly newsletters and has a Web site that with information:.

http://www.mend.org
E-mail   rebekah@mend.org

🙰🙰🙰🙰🙰🙰🙰🙰🙰🙰🙰🙰🙰🙰🙰🙰🙰🙰🙰🙰🙰🙰🙰🙰

SHARE   (800) 821-6819
National Share Pregnancy
   and Infant Loss Support
St. Joseph Health Center
300 First Capital Drive
St. Charles, MO   63012-2893

SHARE is a resource center for bereaved parents. They have support groups throughout the United States. You can call the national office for the telephone number of the support group in your state.

http://www.nationalshareoffice.com
E-mail   share@nationalshareoffice

FOR FAMILIES OF A DECEASED CHILD

THE COMPASSIONATE FRIENDS
National Chapter: (877) 969-0010
P.O. Box 3696, Oak Brook, IL 60522

THE COMPASSIONATE FRIENDS have local chapters with volunteers (themselves bereaved parents) to accept telephone calls.

   http://www.compassionatefriends.org

E-mail: nationaloffice@compassionatefriends.org

A.G.A.S.T   (888) 774-7437
ALLIANCE OF **G**RANDPARENTS
    A SUPPORT IN **T**RAGEDY
2323 N. Central Avenue
Suite 1204
Phoenix, AZ 85004

AGAST supports grandparents, who have suffered the loss of a grandchild, with informational packets, peer contact and newsletters.

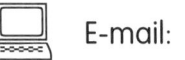

   E-mail: GRANMASIDS@AOL.COM

SIDS ALLIANCE   (800) 221-7437
SUDDEN INFANT DEATH SYNDROME ALLIANCE
1314 Bedford Avenue, Suite 210
Baltimore, MD 21208

The SIDS Alliance is a national, not-for-profit, voluntary organization. Their Web site offers information and the names and E-mail addresses of chapters in all of the states.

        http//www.sidsalliance.org
        E-mail: sidshq@charm.net

FOR FAMILIES OF SUICIDES

AMERICAN ASSOC. OF SUICIDOLOGY
4201 Connecticut Ave. NW, Suite 408
Washington, DC 20008   (202) 237-2280

The American Association of Suicidology is a not-for-profit organization that promotes education, public awareness and research for suicide prevention. It serves as a national clearinghouse for information on suicide. You can call for the number of a support group nearest you. Their Web site has the names, addresses and telephone numbers of organizations that offer counseling to families who have lost a loved one to suicide.

        http://www.suicidology.org

But What If I Can't Stop Grieving?

We noted that there are five stages of grieving:
shock/disbelief,
anger/guilt
searching/pining
sadness/depression
acceptance of the loss.

There is no right way to grieve. You may pass through a stage rapidly or even skip a stage. You may get hung up in one of the stages and have difficulty getting beyond that emotion. Some psychologists refer to this as "stuckness." It's something like what used to happen to 45-rpm phonograph records that were popular in the 1940s and 1950s.

For the benefit of the digital generation who have no experience with phonographs, the record was played by means of a needle that glided over groves of a revolving disk (the record). Sometimes the needle would get stuck in a groove and play the same sound over and over again until the annoyed listener bumped it into the next groove.

If you are stuck in one of the stages of mourning you may think the suggestions in this section to be useless in your situation because they encourage you to be proactive, i.e., to actively seek to help yourself. If you are thinking:

"I **can't** help myself. "

or

"If I could help myself, I wouldn't have this problem," then the first thing you need to understand, and accept, is that you have no other choice but to help yourself. The pain exists within you and no where else. Because the pain is internal and unique to you, only you can ease that pain. This does not mean that no one can help you to deal with the pain. It just means that you need to be interactive with the healing process; and in particular, you need to take the first step.

What is that first step? To answer that question you need to identify those areas of your life with which you are having difficulty. It might help to make a list of all of the things that are bothering you. Once you compose the list, look at the last item on the list. If you are like most people, you will initially avoid thinking about what is really troubling you. It may take the last item on the list for you to admit to yourself what is really causing the problem.

Once you identify the problem, the identification itself should suggest the solution. For example, suppose you find the holidays unbearable, then a solution may be to change your holiday routine. Instead of wearing yourself out shopping for gifts, use the money to treat yourself to a boat cruise. Tell everyone that this year you are taking a holiday from the holidays. You may find that people are just as tired of exchanging gifts as you are and that they gladly welcome the change.

For those who are lonely, the solution will involve companionship. How you find companionship depends on your personality. If you are lonely, but not a social person, consider adopting a pet. For the civic minded, companionship can be found by volunteering for community activities. If you are physically active, then perhaps you can take up a new sport or even pick up a sport that you used to enjoy at an earlier time in your life. If you enjoy sports but are not in the best shape, then consider coaching a team sport for children.

You need to make a conscious effort to concentrate on things in your life that are right, as opposed to thoughts that make you angry or sad. This may be difficult to do. During periods of high stress, you may feel as if your mind has a mind of its own. Thoughts may race through your mind even though you'd just as soon not think them. Prayer and/or meditation may help you to reestablish discipline in your thinking process.

If you find you are unable to take control despite your best efforts, then you may require medical and/or psychological assistance to lift the depression. If you seek medical treatment, then you need to be interactive in the process. You cannot stand passively by saying "Now heal me." Pharmaceutical hyperbole notwithstanding, there is no magic pill. An antidepressant may help you to gain control of yourself, but you still need to come to terms with the loss.

If you feel that you have tried it all and you still are unable to find peace and contentment in your life, then you need to ask the hard question:
"What is it about mourning that I really enjoy?"

Strange question? Not really.

You may enjoy thinking of your loved one even if the thought gives you as much pain as pleasure. You may think that if you stop mourning, then you truly lose the decedent. If that's the case, then compartmentalize your grief, that is, set aside a special time of the day to actively think about and/or grieve for your loved one and the rest of the day not to grieve or even think about the decedent.

Actively plan the grieving compartment of your day. You may wish to have a grieving routine, perhaps visit the grave site once a week; or quietly spend 15 minutes a day looking at pictures of the decedent or writing down your memories of the happy times you had together. If you have been discussing your grief with family or friends, restrict such talks to specific times, perhaps on the decedent's birthday, or on the anniversary of his death.

Set aside as much time each day as you believe you need to mourn, but here is the hard part — you need to exercise self restraint not to mourn, nor talk about, nor even think of the decedent during any other part of the day. If your mind wanders back to the sadness and loneliness of the loss, postpone it. Say to yourself, "Hold that thought till my next grieving compartment."

If you are speaking to someone, do not mention the decedent or how you are feeling about the loss until your scheduled grieving talk with that person. If the subject happens to come up during a conversation, then change the subject by saying "We'll talk about that later."

Hopefully you will find the pain of your loss to lessen over time, in frequency and/or intensity.

It isn't so much that time heals; it is more that you learn to heal yourself over time.

OTHER BOOKS BY AMELIA E. POHL

Attorney Amelia E. Pohl has written a series of books that give guidance to those who have lost a loved one. *Guiding Those Left Behind In . . . (name of state)* explains the legal and practical things a person needs to do when someone dies in the given state. The book explains:

- what agencies to notify of the death
- how to locate the decedent's assets
- what bills do (and do not) need to be paid
- who inherits the property
- whether probate is necessary
- how to transfer property to the proper beneficiary.

The book also contains a section entitled EVERYMAN'S ESTATE PLAN. This chapter explains how a person can arrange his/her own finances so that the family is not burdened with unnecessary costs and hassle. It explains:

- how to avoid probate
- the benefits (and problems) associated with a trust
- how to provide for a minor child
- how to avoid guardianship

and much more.

Each state has its own set of laws relating to the settlement of a person's estate. The author is in the process of "translating" *Guiding Those Left Behind* for each state.

The following books are now in print:

ALABAMA	ARIZONA
CALIFORNIA	FLORIDA
GEORGIA ILLINOIS	INDIANA
MARYLAND	MASSACHUSETTS
MICHIGAN	MINNESOTA
MISSISSIPPI	MISSOURI
NEW JERSEY	NEW YORK
NORTH CAROLINA	OHIO
PENNSYLVANIA	SOUTH CAROLINA
TENNESSEE TEXAS	VIRGINIA
WASHINGTON	WISCONSIN

Check the Eagle Publishing Company Web site: http://www.eaglepublishing.com to determine if the book is now available in other states, or you can call the company at (800) 824-0823.

SPECIAL DISCOUNT COUPON

To order any of the above books, circle the state you wish and mail a copy of this page and a check for $20 for each book to:
EAGLE PUBLISHING COMPANY OF BOCA
4199 N. Dixie Hwy. #2
Boca Raton, FL   33431

THE *Guiding Those Left Behind* SERIES HAS RECEIVED EXCELLENT REVIEWS:

ARIZONA Ben T. Traywick of the Tombstone Epitaph said "This book is an excellent reference book that simplifies all the necessary tasks that must be done when there is a death in the family. There is even an explanation as to how you can arrange your own estate so that your heirs will not be left with a multitude of nagging problems." "This reviewer has been going through probate for two years with no end yet in sight. This book at the beginning two year ago would have helped immensely."

CALIFORNIA Margot Petit Nichols of the Carmel Pine Cone called it a ". . A TRULY RIVETING READ." ". . . . I could scarcely put it down." "This is a book that we should all have, either on our book shelves or thoughtfully placed with our important papers."

FLORIDA Maryhelen Clague of the Tampa Tribune Times wrote "Amelia Pohl has created a handy, self-help guide that illustrates the necessary steps that must be taken when someone dies, a guide that is easy to read, extremely clear and simple to refer to when the need arises."

NEW YORK Saul Friedman of NEWSDAY said "And one section that should be read by readers of any age, suggests and describes how to create an 'If I Die' file to point the way to your vital papers and insurance policies, to minimize the problems and costs for your survivors. Alas, not even you boomers will live forever."